Endless Staircase

ENDLESS STAIRCASE

Sandy McIntosh

For Stefanie,
I've enjoyed meeting you over these last few weeks. Here's to the future!
Sandy McIntosh
May 16, 1992

Street Press
New York

Published by STREET PRESS
Box 772
Sound Beach, New York 11789-0772

Cover design by Betsy Orbe Lester

Some of these poems first appeared in *Bird Effort, Poets and Painters
Scrub Oak, Street Magazine,* and *Survivors' Manual.*

"The Classic", "Rosa-Rosa Gave Me a Kiss", Wedding Song", Nine
Questions Concerning the Refrigerator", Nothing is Clear Before Or
After", The Arnold Schoenberg Monument", "Piano Lessons" and
"December Night" were originally published in "*Monsters of the
Antipodes*

Words to "Birthday Party" by John Thompson from Teaching Little Fingers to Play
Copyright, The Willis Music Co. Used by permission.

The author thanks Charles Matz, Karen Walsh and Janus Lee for
their help in the preparation of this book.

Printed in the United States of America

5 4 3 2 1

ISBN 0-935252-48-7

Table of Contents

1. THE BRUTALITY OF MEMORY

2. VAMPYRE CAMEOS

3. SLEEPER AWAKE

4. ENDLESS STAIRCASE

To the Memory of My Brother
Donald Bane McIntosh
1952 - 1989

1. THE BRUTALITY OF MEMORY

MILITARY MUSIC
for John Atkins

1.
I had been knitting a scarf for several years.
It was fifteen feet long; I didn't know how to end it.
My father wanted me to be a real man
who did not knit scarves,
who could hold his own in a boxing match.
Steps would have to be taken, he argued, soon,
or how would I end up?
Writing poetry?

2.
My father abandoned me to his train of thought
heading for military school.
In the middle of nowhere (nameless rocks,
grass, trees), I jumped from the caboose.
You'll never take me alive, I vowed, never!
Next day we were off to military school
in his car. And that has made
all the difference.

3.
My friends were the oddballs:
Brooks, who defecated in the officers' combat boots,
Ron, whose penis was so big
boys in the showers backed away in awe.
I was at home on the winter parade grounds,
in the empty piano practice rooms, under the trees
along the Hudson where I watched something;
a bird; something.

4.
My father died and backed me into a room full of music.
Chopin was describing one's life: how tangled
the laces of its shoes, how sad the tears in its eyes,
how mindful the knowledge of its impermanence.
I was playing a Chopin waltz in the empty military Chapel
when a teacher said, "That's the most beautiful thing
I've ever heard." Later, he was dismissed
for buggering some kid.

5.
After we'd thrown our hats into the air,
and my friends were drinking whiskey in the Ramble,
I climbed the barracks roof
and threw my dress uniform over the edge.
I heard my friends singing
as the coat spread its wings. It glided
above the trees. It flew like a bird;
a blue shadow; my twin.

6.
Military music is to music. . .
(I was uplifted, floating about the classroom,
the band below playing *Washington Post*.)
. . .as music is to. . .
(I flew to the top of Storm King Mountain.
The sun rose within mine eyes; I beheld its glory.)
. . .as music is to God. . .
(Grace notes.)

THE GENERATOR

"What are you thinking?" asked my wife as we lay around on a Sunday. "It's something I remembered about my father and me, and why I always worry about my art."

On my ninth birthday I had invented the Generator down in my basement laboratory. It was a white cardboard box with dials and wires in front and a toy tractor motor in the back that made the special Generator sound. My friends from school came to my birthday party. Those I wanted to impress I took downstairs to the basement after ice cream and cake. "This is my Generator I invented!" I announced. And I turned the dials to *ON* with one hand while slipping the other behind to turn on the motor.

What a sound it made!

But my friends only laughed. "That's not a generator," they said. "It is, it is!" I pleaded. I could not believe they would not believe me. "Go ask my father."

"Ok," they said, "let's go ask your father." We stood at the bottom of the stairs. "Call your father," they ordered. He stood at the top on the landing. "Daddy," I asked, "isn't it really a Generator?"

My eyes searched my father's face for the secret code, some way to let him know my dilemma. Help me please, Daddy, I begged him on all the silent frequencies.

He was looking at us. Couldn't he see my friends standing behind me, their faces smoldering red, saliva on their fangs?

"Well," my father finally answered, "It certainly generates something."

Oh no, I thought, *oh no.*

My friends laughed at me. I protested, "You don't understand... " But they laughed, and then it was over.

"Anyway," I said to my wife, "I think that is why I wonder so much about my poems. Am I fooling myself again? Can people see inside me where phony motors grind? I wonder and I look hard, but the most I can ever get from the eyes of other people is *yes, they certainly generate something.*

A RELIQUARY

1.
She was the daughter
of my aunt's first piano student.
She showed exceptional
promise (according
to my Aunt).

2.
She was 10. I
was 6.
My Aunt took us
to the Metropolitan Opera
every Saturday.
I learned to sleep
with my head upright,
without snoring,
through beauty, Wagner,
wheat and chaff.

3.
I was 10. It was
her birthday. My mother
bought her a gift in my name. I
wanted to give her something
from me, personally.
I was already
in love with her. But,
it was too late: we were
at a concert. I lied
and told her
I had bought a gift,

and had hidden it under the snow.

After the concert, we dug and dug,
but the gift
was nowhere to be found.

4.
I was sent to boarding school.
She was a high school senior
engaged to a football hero.
He was killed in a car accident.
She attended Vassar,
became the first woman
student at Harvard.

We exchanged letters
on philosophical
questions. I faked it;
she seemed to know
what she was talking about.

5.
She married a French lawyer. They
lived in Paris. She taught
at the Sorbonne. Her husband
died after a fall
on their apartment stairs.
She was consoled by his best friend,
a Vietnamese. They were
to be married
after his final trip to Saigon.
Two years passed without
a word from him. She

returned to the States.

6.
She worked at the U.N.
as a translator. I was married
and taught college.
Within a year she was engaged
to a young Russian, great-nephew
of the late Czar. They moved
into a mansion
purchased with her family's money.

She gave a dinner party.
Everyone there had a Ph.D.
except my wife.
During a ponderous silence
we all stared
at my wife.

7.
She had two children,
twin girls. Her husband
seemed healthy,
not prone to accidents.
Two years passed.
One day she called to tell me
one of her daughters
had tested out
a genius; the other
seemed marginally retarded.
They needed a special school.
My friend planned to sell
their mansion

and move to the city.
She herself
suffered from lupus,
an incurable disease.

8.
An old friend of my Aunt
told us the rest:
My friend
had died in horrible
pain. Her body was cremated
or buried (my Aunt's
friend didn't know which)
privately.
Her Russian husband
had wandered off in his grief.
Her twin daughters
now lived with their grandmother.

9.
My wife and I divorced
unpleasantly (although
I remember how
we cried in each other's arms
with the knowledge
that something we had borne
had died).

Religion in the next century
must teach us joy
in the abandonment
of the useless search for meaning.

BEACH PLUMS IN LATE SEPTEMBER
for David and Rose

After a short trip to the country he stopped at his teacher's house. It was the end of September and the beach plums hanging from their branches were purple and ripe. He'd brought a new poem for the teacher's approval, a piece he was especially proud of. The teacher was a well-known poet who commuted daily to a teaching job in the city. He was not home.

The teacher's wife asked him to wait. She poured a cup of herbal tea for him from the teapot on the kitchen table. She showed him her new project: a group of drawings of local poets soon to be published. He was too new a writer to be included in the series. "But who knows?" she told him. "Next time you'll be published and I'll immortalize you."

From the painting studio at the back of the house the voice of a radio newscaster announced the death of President Eisenhower. The teacher's wife remarked how chilling it was: Eisenhower dead less than an hour and already the announcer reading the complex plans for a funeral that must have taken months to prepare. "They couldn't wait for him to drop dead," she said.

He knew he'd have to wait a few hours for the teacher's return, so he begged a typewriter. He'd had an idea for a poem about Eisenhower. She told him to go ahead, type all you want.

His father had admired Eisenhower and always voted Republican. At his father's death some years before, he'd been fascinated with the preparations for the funeral, especially the process of embalming the corpse. He was thinking as much of his own father as of Eisenhower while he worked at the teacher's typewriter.

The teacher returned in the evening by a late train. He was in an acrimonious mood and said nothing as he ate his austere supper (canned salmon on dry lettuce; water).

"Alright," said the teacher when he had finished eating. "Show me what you've brought."

He presented the poem he'd worked on for weeks, that he was proudest of. The teacher coughed several times as he read it, and made chomping sounds as he cleaned his teeth with his tongue. He looked up with a sour expression.

"This is trash," the teacher pronounced. "Why are you wasting your time with this garbage? You can write better than that."

He was devastated. He couldn't breathe. He felt as if he'd been shoved backwards through the wall; that he was pinned somewhere within the airless beams of the house.

"Come on," the teacher said. "You can talk. You're not going to die."

He couldn't talk, the teacher's condemnation so forceful and unexpected. To play for time, he opened his notebook and offered up the new poem about Eisenhower. The teacher grabbed at it. His expression softened slowly as he read. He looked up.

"Now, this is something," said the teacher. "This should be published. Why didn't you show me this the first time?"

THE CLASSIC

"When your daughter was fourteen,"
I told the old poet,
"she was so smart I had to lie
to win philosophical arguments against her."

He laughed.
He was pleased.
"That's a classic story,
That's really a classic."

"You always lie. . ."

What?
The young poet sitting next to me
had said something
under his breath.
Was that it? "You always lie?"

Well, it was true. Something strange
inside me
wants always to shape, always to craft.

I wanted to tell him he was right,
it had happened again:
Even the story I had just told him
was a lie.

THE SOCIAL FUNCTION OF POETRY
for Frank and Billie

He had read Eliot's "The Social Function of Poetry," Ezra Pound's letters, and the essays of William Carlos Williams. He was ready to fight for poetry's place. He was teaching poetry to children in the public schools, and wanted to convince them that poetry offered something powerful for their lives.

Meanwhile, a friend from graduate school called. The friend worked for a public relations firm and needed some genuine Irish poetry for a film about Dublin. The poetry, said his friend, must extol the beauty of the land, the vitality of the people, and the rapid growth of industrial production.

He spent an afternoon searching the library's anthologies. Not surprisingly, he found nothing answering the requirements. All Irish poetry was depression. In the end, only one appeared reasonably upbeat. It began:

Thank God, I've left Ireland forever!

His friend told him not to give up. He needed the material; his job depended upon it. He named the famous Irish-American television actor contracted to read the verses in the film. "Go back to the library," begged his friend. "You've got to help me out of this jam."

He tried another library without success. In the end, he decided to forge it, to create an ancient Irish poem to order.

To his surprise, it was easy: All he had to do was imagine an ancient village scene and voice it in Yeatsian accent. In a short time, the rhymed stanzas appeared fully-formed, like photographs in a chemical bath.

In the deep musical voice of the film's famous narrator, the verses and pictures became powerfully fused. The first scene: quiet, leafy trees. Swans preening upon the rustic pond. The second scene: The camera pulls back. The pond is ringed by a cobble-stone square. Dubliners of all ages, happy and vigorous, stride by. The third scene: The camera pulls back again. The street is at the center of a modern industrial city. Within the blue skies of this diorama, smoke curls contentedly from the chimneys.

His friend was delighted, the project completed, the sponsor happy, and the film honored at a film festival. Later, he returned to the public schools, looking for poetry's place.

BLACK STONE
for Dolly

At their last meeting, she gave him a stone. Small and black with flakes of bright crystal, it fit the palm of his hand. "Keep this," she told him, "I've been walking around with it for a month. It has me all over it."

He accepted it greedily. She was the loveliest woman he had ever known, and holding the stone, he tried to absorb all of her through his palm.

Ten years later they met by accident in another city. She was still lovely, married a second time, with a small baby. He showed her the stone.

"You told me if I kept this you'd always be with me."

"Ah," she said looking at the stone. "Did I really? What a funny thing to have told you."

THE BRUTALITY OF MEMORY

"I don't remember this one," I said to my old friend as we looked over photographs. In this one I am wearing a Superman costume, standing next to some garbage cans. "You don't remember how you convinced my little brother you could fly over our house?" asked my friend. "You did," she insisted. "You and Willy were out back and you said, 'Willy, I can fly over the roof,' and you made Willy close his eyes, and you said, 'Don't open them 'til I tell you,' and you snuck around the house. When you got there, you yelled for Willy to open his eyes. And when he saw you weren't there he ran around the house. And there you were! 'See, I flew over the house,' you said, and Willy believed you did just that."

I thought about Willy as he is today and felt a stab. "I feel guilty about him," I told my friend. "I think I helped start his fall from grace."

"Don't worry about it," she said, "he takes care of himself." Willy hangs around the street lights, selling drugs cut beyond usefulness or recognition. His goal is to make two thousand dollars a day. "Then I can retire," he boasts. He sneaks from shadow to shadow; he lifts them up like manhole covers and climbs beneath the earth.

Somehow, I remain convinced I was the first to push him too far. And I am not relieved on occasions when I walk into the street and he catches my eye, and offers me a little something to smoke or swallow, and when he says, "Try some of these: they'll really make you fly!"

2. VAMPYRE CAMEOS

VAMPYRE CAMEOS
for Jeffrey Goldwasser

The young vampyre
makes homely women beautiful
by his love. He showers them with gifts.
He dances in weird, fire-lit imagination.
He thanks his good fortune,
but soon becomes empty,
vacant as a swimming pool in autumn.

The vampyre in middle age
makes homely women homelier.
His gifts become cloying: bits of string,
his false teeth. . . He dances before them,
but his victims retreat. He persists,
but his thoughts wander. His eyes
lose hypnotic power.

The senile vampyre
is captured by homely women
and taken in hand. They mend his dress suit.
They brush his top hat. They stuff
his hollow body with rags and make him dance
the new steps. The vampyre believes his love
has made him young. He longs to wander
back alleys, but his lovers sew him
into a banner which they hang
above the castle door. There he flaps
like a bat every night in the rain,
flaps himself into shreds,
then flaps no more.

FOR DORA B. (I)
(On First Looking Into Her Eyes)

I am two men
on two small boats
on two blue lakes.
I rest my selves against the oars.
Beneath my boats the tides
echo and answer, answer and echo.
Who could have known how pleasant
these waters,
how effortless this feat,
this being at peace with myself
in two places at once?

FOR DORA B. (II)

She was a beautiful woman, and she kept looking into his eyes. She was that rare person who attends poetry readings but does not herself write poems.

She had been to school in Paris and modeled in her spare time. (Once Salvador Dali invited her to pose. He did not actually paint her. He just asked to see her breasts, stared at them for several minutes, thanked her cheerfully and departed.) She spoke French well. She was bright and had made a successful career in public relations.

They met a week later at the beach and talked for a long time. In a couple of days, she told him, she would turn forty. She was apprehensive. What would it be like, that dark age? A long tunnel to nowhere? No, she would not have wine at dinner. She had once been alcoholic, and spent most evenings with an alcoholic support group. She would have to do this for the rest of her life, she thought, but it wasn't so bad: at least you met nice people with similar interests.

He cooked dinner for them while she took a nap on his bed. (Later she told him, "You can brag to your friends you got me into bed on the first date." "That's nothing," he answered. "I usually get married on the first date.") He poured himself a glass of wine while he cooked, being as quiet as possible. He felt guilty: he didn't want her to hear the draw of the cork, the glug of the pouring liquid. At dinner she told him to go ahead, drink some wine, it didn't bother her. He drank a glass openly but couldn't stop imagining how he must look to her: not holding crystal, but a little bottle in a brown bag, sprawled on the sidewalk in a pool of urine, his fly open, a drooling lush.

After dinner she tried on some hats from his collection at the front door. In one she imitated a little girl, pouting. In another, a vivacious, sophisticated lady. But in his straw hat she looked terrifying: a profile thin as shadow, stiletto nose, death-ray eyes. Someone who could eviscerate you with aplomb. Who could chew you up and spit you out.

They had a date for another poetry reading, but that afternoon he called to cancel out. "I've had a tiring day," he told her, "and sometimes the city seems so far off." She was at the office and couldn't talk. She went to the reading without him, even asking the poet to autograph the book of poems he'd lent her. He called to apologize, but she let him have it:

"You're a manipulator," she declared. "I'm not used to being treated this way. I don't know if I can forgive you."

They left it that she would call him if and when he was forgiven.

Several weeks later she still hadn't called.

ADMONITION (I)

As you enter the room
I rise up and balance on one toe!
It is you who have inspired
this graceful moment.
But it doesn't mean anything to you.
You are too young and too stupid,
and you've never had to struggle
for anything
ever in your life.
"Come on, now," you shout.
"You're being silly!
Stop acting like a fairy!

ADMONITION (II)

"I couldn't stop myself," my old professor told me with an embarrassed smile. "You know how it is with these young girls."

He had taken her home one night when his wife was away on a trip. She was under twenty, an Italian from the Bronx. They had been flirting for a month when she dared him: "It's now or never ever," she said.

They stayed up late drinking wine and smoking marijuana in the dark bedroom. They kissed a long time under the covers. She had never done anything like this before, she told him. She asked to use the phone. He heard her in the next room.

"Yeah, I'm really here, in bed with my teacher," she was saying in a strident voice. "Do you want me to prove it? I'll let you talk to him!" She dropped the phone and ran to the bedroom. "My cousin wants to talk to you. He doesn't believe you're my teacher and that you're married and I'm in bed with you. Will you tell him you are?"

"No, of course not!" He said. "Are you crazy?"

She made a face and returned to the telephone. "He can't talk to you right now," she said. "But I'm really here. I am, too!" And she hung up abruptly.

She was sulky the rest of the night. He kept anticipating loud knocks at the front door. The next morning he woke with a headache.

Silently sleeping in the early light, she wasn't pretty at all. She looked like a corpse. He imagined digging a hole for her in the backyard. He touched her shoulder with his fingers as a kind of test. He felt an unpleasant ripple in his stomach.

She wanted a big breakfast, and he made it for her and brought it to her in bed. He opened the train schedule, but she made a face. "You promised to drive me home!" she said.

He was able to sneak her out of the house before his neighbors saw anything. There was traffic all the way to the Bronx. She wanted to see him again. She thought she might be in love. Would last night help her get a better grade? What if she were pregnant? She wondered when she could meet his wife.

It was a hot day. The drive there lasted forever. The drive home was only somewhat better, accomplished as it was in humid, unpleasant silence.

DELICIOUS (I)

After we had been kissing for a long time
I could see your lips had swelled and purpled
like ripe plums.

I confess: I've never seen ripe plums before,
but I believe I will be able
to recognize them now.

DELICIOUS (II)

They hadn't seen each other for several years. He was divorced; she had recently abandoned a difficult relationship. The friend who passed on the information was worried. "Be careful," said his friend. "She's had a rough time and so have you. Don't get too close too fast." But he ignored his friend and took her with him on a business trip to San Francisco.

For him, the first days were idyllic:

As we lay together
in the early light
I photographed each cell of your skin
with my skin.
I opened my pores and breathed
every inch of you in.
I have never felt this greedy before.

For her, the present was a traffic intersection of urgency and confusion:

Does the woman in the circle hold a square?
Does the square
hang a triangular sign
around her neck that says,
"No trespassing"?

The woman wants the game to end!
The circles, squares and all
forbidding signs
to go away.

*A headache is coming
around the block.
Now she chops away at it.*

One afternoon they returned to the hotel from a trip to
Fisherman's Wharf. She wore a shiny silk scarf; he wore
a "49'ers" straw hat with silver bells depending from the
brim. The bells gave a jangly, pleasant ring.

He thought it would be fun to call his answering machine
in New York. She thought so, too. They pushed their
heads together to share the telephone.

There were several calls. A woman with a squeaky voice
offered magazine subscriptions. A plumber called about
an overdue bill. An artist friend talked on and on about
his troubles, eventually sighing, "It's been great talking
with you!"

Then a final call: A timorous male voice, barely audible.
"Uh, hello?" Said the voice. "Hello? This is Philip. I'm
Jane's boyfriend. Or, uh, at least I used to be. I'm trying
to find her. No one will tell me where she is. They're all
lying to me! I know she's there! Tell her to call me.
Please."

She began to moan: "Oh, it's Philip! Oh, what's happened
to Philip! I have to call Philip. Poor Philip's in trouble."

"All right," he answered her, panicked. "It's ok. Call him."

She called, but there was no trouble; Philip was just lone-
ly. She talked and talked into the telephone. Meanwhile,

he had been sitting on the bed next to her. She spoke urgently, intimately, oblivious of him. He moved to the bathroom to be out of earshot.

The call seemed endless. Finally enraged, he grabbed his straw hat and left the hotel. He found the beach and huddled against a jetty wall, shaking with anger. She had sounded so happy talking to Philip; her hazy state of mind at last resolved.

People passing by stared at him. He growled and stared back with murderous intent. He must have been a figure difficult to pass without a second glance: a man in obvious distress, wearing a silly hat with bells ringing as he shook.

SQUARING THE CIRCLE

Take me to lunch, she said.
Why should I, he said.
Because I touched your dick, she said.
That was for your benefit, he said.
I've heard that before, she said.
Hundreds of times, I'll bet, he said.
But I never touched
such an old one, she said.
Because you hang around schoolyards, he said.
You probably can't keep it up for an hour,
she said. Men never can, she said.
They come too fast, she said.
They want to get it over with, he said.
With my luck, she said, you'll turn out
to be a forty-year old premature ejaculator.
Thanks a lot, he said.
Don't mention it, she said.

     * * *

That's a terrible poem, she said.
Well, I wrote every word we said, he said.
And you made your lines funnier
than mine, she said.
But you win all the same
in the end, he said.
Well, I'm not saying another word
you can steal, she said. And, goddamn it,
put down that pencil when I'm talking.

MS. S. ASSESSES HER BOYFRIEND

On the plus side
he has money, she thinks.
But on the negative,
his lips are too small.
(Once, his whole head
fell into her mouth.)

THE SUNDAY COMICS
for Suzanne

1.
Punch and Judy are driving to the city
in Judy's Land Rover.
Judy asks Punch: "Will you always
be honest with me?"
Punch replies: "I'll be honest,
but discreet!"

2.
Judy turns on him menacingly.
"What da ya mean by that?" demands Judy.
Punch answers: "Not everyone
will be happy knowing everything!"
Judy retorts: "You *had better* tell *me*
everything!"

3.
Punch and Judy at home.
The mailman, winking, hands Punch
a letter. It's from an old girlfriend.
"Dear Punch," writes the girlfriend.
"I'm dripping with lust for you!
I want you to make love to me
every day for a whole year!"
Punch quickly hides the letter.

4.
Judy demands: "What came in the mail?"
Punch hesitates, then hands her
the letter. Judy reads it.

She screams: "*Arrrrrrrrrrrrrrrrrrgh!*"
and grabs her rolling pin.

5.
Judy is chasing Punch down the street,
swinging the rolling pin over her head.
"*You sneaking son-of-a-bitch!*" screams Judy,
"*You're gonna be sorry you were ever born!*"

"Oh God!" cries Punch.
"I knew discretion was better
than honesty!"

ROSA-ROSA GAVE ME A KISS
(and What Happened Thereafter)

Rosa-Rosa gave me a kiss which covered up my lips
and slid around my chin and jumped into my shirt
on its two spider legs.

I tried to grab that awful kiss but it hid in my armpit,
and I could not grab it when it ran down my back.

So I screamed, and stunned it with my scream
when it got caught in the belt of my pants,
and I threw it back in Rosa-Rosa's face.

It hit her mouth, but not exact, and it stained her red
like a spider bite.

Rosa-Rosa looked at me so sadly
I put my arms around her
and she leaned against my shoulder.

And as we stood that way, her lips parted
and her two teeth bit into me. And ever since,
whenever I kiss some woman,
those lips hiss and spit at her,
and sometimes the woman runs away.
And that is why I do not get
too many kisses
anymore.

JUDGEMENT DREAM

I was in Ireland.
Cathy was holding court.
A man my own age rose to speak.
He pointed his finger at me.
"Who is that man? He demanded.
"Is there still room for me?"
"Of course there is," Cathy answered
with gentle smile, measured voice.
"We will see each other often."
"And me?" I pleaded, mortified.
"What about me?"
"Oh, Sandy," she said, "Nothing has changed
between us."
My rival rose to go. He embraced me
and called me his brother.
I said nothing at all.
An old woman huddled in a corner crying.
"What is wrong, Mother?" I asked.
She raised her eyes and said,
"I thought death itself
was the ultimate judge. Not Cathy."

WEDDING SONG

Let us grow together
and be known as the Strange Thing
or, the Living Rock.
And let bright creatures
come forth from our caves.

Let us become craggy
and be called grandmother and grandfather.
And let your name be mine
and mine be yours, and let our secrets
stay secrets.

Let us become inseparable
and spin through space
and be anonymous as a comet
that appears once a thousand years.
And when we are seen rolling
through the air, and when someone asks
our name, let him wander
and ask others, and let him wonder,
but let him never find out.

3. SLEEPER AWAKE

NINE QUESTIONS CONCERNING
THE REFRIGERATOR

The refrigerator purrs and mews.
Will she try to curl up in the cook's lap
while he snoozes under his book?
Will she shudder in defeat
like a retarded child who does not understand
her enormous size?

She certainly is the pet of the kitchen.
We stroke her and stuff her with food.
Do we think she is our mother?
Is this why we might find a child curled up
behind the rusted door
of an abandoned refrigerator?

We know that when the kitchen light
is turned off she whimpers and howls.
She tugs at her leash plugged into the wall.
If she got free would she wander the house
looking for the cook's bed?
Would she crawl in beside the cook,
lay her door across his shoulder?
Would the cook grunt and roll over
like a husband making room
for his wife?

NOTHING IS CLEAR BEFORE OR AFTER

Nothing is clear, before or after. I had found a poet whose work I liked, liked, perhaps, too much. I was fascinated. I wanted to tell him how much I liked his work, to ask him embarrassing questions that would probably embarrass me and leave him non-plussed.

(Once, I had called my favorite writer, P.G. Wodehouse, on the phone. His wife said he was watching the news. I said I'd only take a minute. He came to the phone and I told him how much I loved his books, and how many hours of pleasure. He thanked me. I told him again. He thanked me again. I began to tell him a third time and he said *Thank you* and hung up the phone. So you see why I am so leery.)

Instead of calling the poet I decided to read the poems again looking for the fatal flaw. At last I thought I had found one. Then I found another. As the weeks went by I found several more. And then, today, I realized his entire conception of poetry is wrong. I've freed myself at last from this compelling fascination.

You'd think this knowledge would make a difference, another step up the rung towards Enlightenment. But no, nothing is clear, not before, not after.

OF LOCAL INTEREST
(Signa Gallery Retrospective,
East Hampton, Summer 1990)

Someone has rolled the stone
from Jackson Pollack's grave.
Albert Price's strange sculptures
have landed next door
like an invasion force from outer space.
It must be 1957 again. The air, the land,
the waters are clean. Several painters
have recently learned to fall from their bicycles.
Few of us have yet committed the mortal sin
that will career us over cliffs
or into divorce courts.
An odd kind of silence spreads itself
upon the land,
as if the air were no longer filled
with television antennas.
Ten or twenty boulders
tumble down Old Stone Highway
like a delinquent motorcycle gang.
They pick up speed.
No one needs to be told:
The Abstract Expressionists are at it again.

DAYDREAM OF THE ADJUNCT
ASSISTANT PROFESSOR

At Southampton seashore
when no one was around,
I saw the Manhattan skyline rise
out of the sea
on enormous, clanging wheels.
I threw stones at it. I raised the alarm,
but no one would listen.
Before I could stop it,
it had reached the college
and eaten the English Department.
From the tallest windows, English professors
spewed and drifted down,
empty as handkerchiefs.

I was the only survivor.

BOSWELL'S MODERN DIARY

This morning, as I drove away
from our local diner,
I saw a man heavy-hung with muscles
cross the road in front of me.
Across his back he wore a black shirt
with the printed word, STROKE, upon it.
I puzzled: Was this the man's name?
Could it be the name
of a rock band or bowling team?
Or, was it something in the nature
of an announcement or proclamation,
that here was a man who
Demands To Be Stroked?
Or, most terrible, could this word
have been following the man
around unbeknownst to him?
Was this the stigmata, the portent
of neurological "accident"
about to occur?
These possibilities flashed through my brain
in a second; but the man
had already disappeared into the crowd
of early morning browsers and shoppers.
Too late for me to warn him.

THE ARNOLD SCHOENBERG MONUMENT

The new science found a use
for musical devices. Dissonance
made the best fuel for tanks and rockets.
A tone-cluster could fire a human to the moon
and back again in moments.
The Twelve-tone system of composition
was studied by the Ministry of War.
The name Ernst Krenek was whispered
in mystical circles.

Soon it was found that machines themselves
were not necessary. The only thing
people had to do to go from place to place
was hum a minor seventh
and close their eyes.
To get back, they had to sing a major second.
A perfect fifth got the shopping done
while a retrograde row
slowed the aging process.

In the capital city the new science
unveiled the Schoenberg Monument.
It is carved from white marble and it shows
the figure of Schoenberg at the center
holding the Tablets of the Law.
Behind him and leaning slightly
over each shoulder are Berg and Webern
with angel wings and cherubic smiles.

OF STRANGE LANDS AND PEOPLE

I don't want to play this piece anymore," my favorite piano student said to me. "It's dead baby music. When I play it, all I think of is dead babies!"

It was "Of Strange Lands And People" by Robert Schumann. "All I think about when I hear it is Schumann throwing dead babies off a bridge. And then I see them bunched together on the ground like plastic dolls!"

I could not argue against her. She was rightly intuitive: There is a weakness in Schumann that abides the hundred years between his times and our own; that stretches like telegraph line connecting his heart at one end, and the music we play at the other. When we tap on the keys, the coded message gets through.

Schumann went insane. He threw himself off a bridge into the River Seine. He died later in an insane asylum with his bed-clothes bunched about him.

Dead baby music.

PRAYER OF THE MAUSOLEUM

He dreamt he was trapped
in his father's mausoleum.
This was no scene
a father should show his son:
the horrible corpse
pleading: "I was not done with the world!"
The bloodless grasping fingers,
the airless night.
Oh lovely world, do not forsake us.
Without others, there is no satisfaction.

A BIRTHDAY POEM
FOR H.R. HAYS

Three hundred sixty bones in the body,
and each is named Monday, Tuesday,
Wednesday . . .
O, my friend, my teacher of old,
you take mysterious comfort in me these days.

This hospital is like a delicatessen window:
toothpicks for a toothless cannibal . . .

Now your eyes are wonderful:
as if lightning had come down
from you hair or
up from your feet into them.
They seem to have taken a step outward
to look at the world on their own.

O, what is the life of the world to come?

PIANO LESSONS

(spoken) My aunt curled her fingers over mine
and they sank into the piano keys.
My first piece, "Birthday Party."
It goes:

(sung) C,D,E. C,D,E. D,C, D,E, C,C.

(spoken) It goes:
(sung) Here we go,
up a row,
to a
birth-
day
par-
ty.

(spoken) The keys are ivory, made of an
elephant's big teeth.
Between the keys
is a white jungle, with tall white trees
and a long white river,
and in the river are Indian boys
washing an elephant
and they are singing:

(sung) Here we go,
up a row,
to a
birth- day par-
ty.

DECEMBER NIGHT

Dear Aunt, when the first snow fell tonight
I thought of you sadly.
It was because, as the snow
covered your grave
I knew it had ended your last battle
on this earth.   .
Your grave has become as white
and anonymous
as the graves of my grandparents
that surround you.
Each winter the snow rubs against the graves
until all below are rubbed out.
Dear Aunt, I see you now
as I have never seen you,
but as I think I must each year hereafter:
only once, and in the winter,
and under the light
of the first falling snow.

SLEEPER AWAKE

My dead aunt returned.
I hid beneath the window.
This had been her house;
now it was mine.
She wandered across the street.
No one answered the door.
I saw shadows
against the curtains.
Awake from a long dream, my aunt
was home. Where was everyone?
The sleeper awake,
the living in darkness beyond.

4. ENDLESS STAIRCASE

ENDLESS STAIRCASE (I)

Of my brother's death
I imagine two things:
I see him in blue empyrean,
skidding and dipping his toes
into the misted river,
combing the flirtatious waters.
The temptation to slip over the edge,
to roll up the eyes, to be gone, to dissolve,
to disintegrate like a pearl in wine.
And I see myself on the morgue's
endless staircase,
the dark wind pushing against me,
pushing with such force
I cannot reach the door.
And, indeed, a year later, I see myself
descending those stairs, as if this descent
had become my whole road.

ENDLESS STAIRCASE (II)

I had agreed to identify my brother's body at the morgue because there was no one else except my mother to do it. There was no way out. I had asked my best friend to go with me as a favor of ultimate loyalty and friendship. My friend agreed.

Queens County Hospital complex is perpetually busy. All sorts of people walk the streets or pass through the buildings. Some have their arms in slings. Others walk with crutches or ride wheelchairs. Some are bent over, walking slowly. A few gesticulate vigorously and direct traffic or debate invisible antagonists.

The Mortuary operates in building "H" of the complex. It stands at the end of the road, next to the laundry. Inside, there are several bolted doors marked "No Admittance" and two open office cubicles.

I stepped into the first and waited for the clerk to finish her long telephone call. Then I spoke the horrible words: "I'm here to identify my brother's body."

The clerk pointed without interest to the next office. "Over there," she said.

I turned and repeated what I had to say. The young woman behind the glass partition asked me to sit and wait. She, too, was on the phone.

"I'm sorry, Mr. Rodriguez," she was saying. "The body you're looking for isn't here. No. Why don't you try the

Manhattan Medical Examiner? Oh, I see. Well, how about Jacoby in the Bronx? Yes? Well, I'm sorry, we can't help you. Um-hmm. You too. Good luck."

She returned to the cubicle where I sat with my friend.

"May I see your identification?"

I fumbled for my driver's license.

"Your relationship to the deceased?

I told her.

"Did the deceased use drugs?

I told her which ones.

"It is necessary at this time," she said, "to identify the body. Wait here."

She picked up her clipboard and left the room.

My brother and I had never been close. I was born healthy and grew up to play in the streets with my friends. My brother's exact birthdate was never resolved. He was born with his fingers and toes webbed like a duck's. They had to be separated surgically. A private nurse raised him in a hermetic world.

I was the obnoxious little boy who spoiled the magician's trick by exposing the cake pan's false bottom. My brother laughed and applauded my magic. I was the one who pulled a policeman's gun from his holster. My brother thought it wonderful, convinced of my immortality. In family photographs we are at the beach, wearing party hats, puffing at corn-cob pipes; we are seated at the big piano playing duets. My brother followed me everywhere.

My father enrolled us in a progressive school where children learned French and German, baking, sewing, interpretive dancing and candle-dipping. After a few years, my father became unhappy and transferred us to separate schools.

At military school I grew up with the nephews of Latin American dictators, the sons of Mafiosi; those constrained by their fathers to learn obedience as well as command. I became solitary, socially uncertain. I learned to love classical music, wrote desperate poems, and avoided athletics.

My brother did well in public school. He had many friends, his grades were good, and he could run fast enough to win track meets. He got into serious trouble once only, when the police stopped his car to find drugs. He was let go after his friends testified against each other in a shoot-out arranged by lawyers.

At eighteen I attended a suburban college. My brother followed me there. I edited the school weekly; a few years later he won the same position.

At twenty-two I went on to a Masters program; my brother changed course and married the girl he had been living with.

His wife was an intelligent person who had been hospitalized eighty times before age eighteen. She had the demanding personality of an invalid. My brother joined the Army to pay his wife's health insurance. After two months he was discharged because of bleeding ulcers. He returned to his wife, and they separated. He left for Colorado.

I ran my aunt's music school for several years, taught poetry in the schools, became a Buddhist, finished my doctorate, taught college, took a job in publishing, then in computer software. I continued writing and publishing poems. I heard little from my brother. During one of our infrequent telephone calls he confided he had been drinking and using drugs. He worked as a guard in an atomic energy plant near Denver. During a power failure he had blown up the house he was renting because he had lit a match to find out what was wrong with the gas furnace. After a near-fatal car crash, he returned home to live with my mother.

During those years he was angry and argumentative. He drank and used drugs to excess. Once, my mother showed me the evidence: syringes and sterile wipes. He told me he was giving himself vitamin injections. His last girlfriend, a patient woman, asked him not to return to her house. "He was drinking and saying crazy things that scared my children," she told me. "He's such a lovely, brilliant man. Why does he do this to himself?"

He moved from one job to another. He clerked in a department store, sold insurance, and ended as a hospital security guard. But he also enrolled in an MBA program, and after an abandoned semester, completed the degree.

On the last Christmas of his life, my brother invited me to his room after dinner. "Here," he said, offering me a small mirror on which familiar white lines were spread. "Check this out." I looked at the powder a second time, its color and texture different than anything I'd seen before.

"What is it?" I asked him.

"Don't you know?" He answered in a superior voice. "Just try it."

"What is it?" I asked again.

He moved close to me and looked into my eyes. I looked back. There was something in his smile I had never seen before: a smirking, alien presence relishing my astonishment.

"Its heroin," he announced triumphantly. "You're afraid of it, I can tell."

"Why are you using heroin?" I demanded.

"It's none of your business," he said.

The clerk returned to the office where my friend and I waited. She was carrying a manilla envelope.

"You'll identify the body by looking at a photograph."

She opened the envelope and from it drew two Polaroids. She held them with their backs facing out. At length, she chose one and turned it decisively, as if it were a Tarot card.

It was a picture of my brother, his head only, wrapped in a white sheet. His eyes were closed, his face bruised. There was blood on his lips and chin. The sneer, the public swagger my brother wore, was gone. I thought of my mother's words earlier that morning and echoed them aloud, "That poor little boy."

To my friend, the corpse looked naive, surprised to be dead.

I said to myself, "That poor little boy," and tears filled my eyes. My friend put his arm around my shoulders.

In the car driving home I told my friend, "I'm going to tell my mother that my brother looked peaceful."

It wasn't true, but that's what I told her.

FAREWELL DREAM

I was visiting my brother's bedroom.
He was hiding under the mattress.
His hideout smelled of sweat.
He was cataloging business cards collected
on a recent trip to Europe.
I felt it was my duty
to tell him he was dead.
Officious, self-appointed scum! I reproached
myself. But who else would tell him?
"You're dead, Donny," I said.
He looked into my eyes; he
couldn't avoid them, trapped where he was.
"How did it happen?" He asked.
"An overdose," I told him. "Like Lenny Bruce,"
"I see," he replied. "I'll just stay in here
by myself a little longer, if you don't mind."
"Ok," I said. "Go ahead. Do whatever you want."
I stood up and took a deep breath.
At last he knew the truth. At last
He had listened to me.

Sandy McIntosh has published poetry in *The Nation*, *Chelsea*, and elsewhere, in addition to three previous collections, *Earth Works* (1970), *Which Way to the Egress?* (1974), and *Monsters of the Antipodes* (1980). He has been a consultant in the teaching of poetry writing to the New York Foundation for the Arts, and his honors include a Silver Medal from the *Film Festival of the Americas* for original poetry in a documentary film. He teaches creative writing at Hofstra University.

Betsy Orbe Lester (cover) is an artist from Treasure Island, Florida.

Street Press, begun in 1973, has published the poetry of William Heyen, Jonathan Cohen, Vince Clemente, Robert Long, Claire Nicholas White, David Ignatow, Norbert Krapf, Michele Cusumano, Dan Murray, John Logan, Michael Braude, Si Perchik, Shreela Ray, Louis Simpson, Allen Planz, Ray Freed, Bonnie Gordon, Lynne Savitt, Leonard Greco, Marge Miller, and Allen Hoey, among others. The Press has also published two major anthologies. John Strausbaugh, writing in the Baltimore *City Paper,* called Street Press "a great example of a small press which has remained true to its regional roots, while branching out to reach a much broader audience."